YPS

Sweet as a Strawberry!

For Tim and Joe for all their help

First published in paperback in 2005 by Zero To Ten,
a division of Evans Brothers Ltd, 2A Portman Mansions,
Chiltern St, London WIU 6NR

Publisher: Anna McQuinn
Art Director: Tim Foster
Senior Editor: Simona Sideri
Publishing Assistant: Vikram Parashar

A CIP catalogue record for this book is available from the British Library.

ISBN 1-84089-415-6

Printed in China

Picture credits
A-Z Botanical Collection: coconut; Holt Studios: banana, sultanas, strawberry;
Photos Horticultural: kiwi fruit, apple, lemon; Pictor: pineapple.

Sally Smallwood

Sweet as a Strawberry!

pineapple

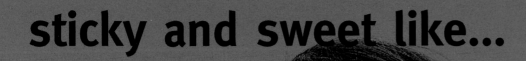

sticky and sweet like...

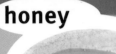

honey

dates

chunk

slice

chunk

sweet

leaf

prickly skin

kiwi fruit

different and delicious like...

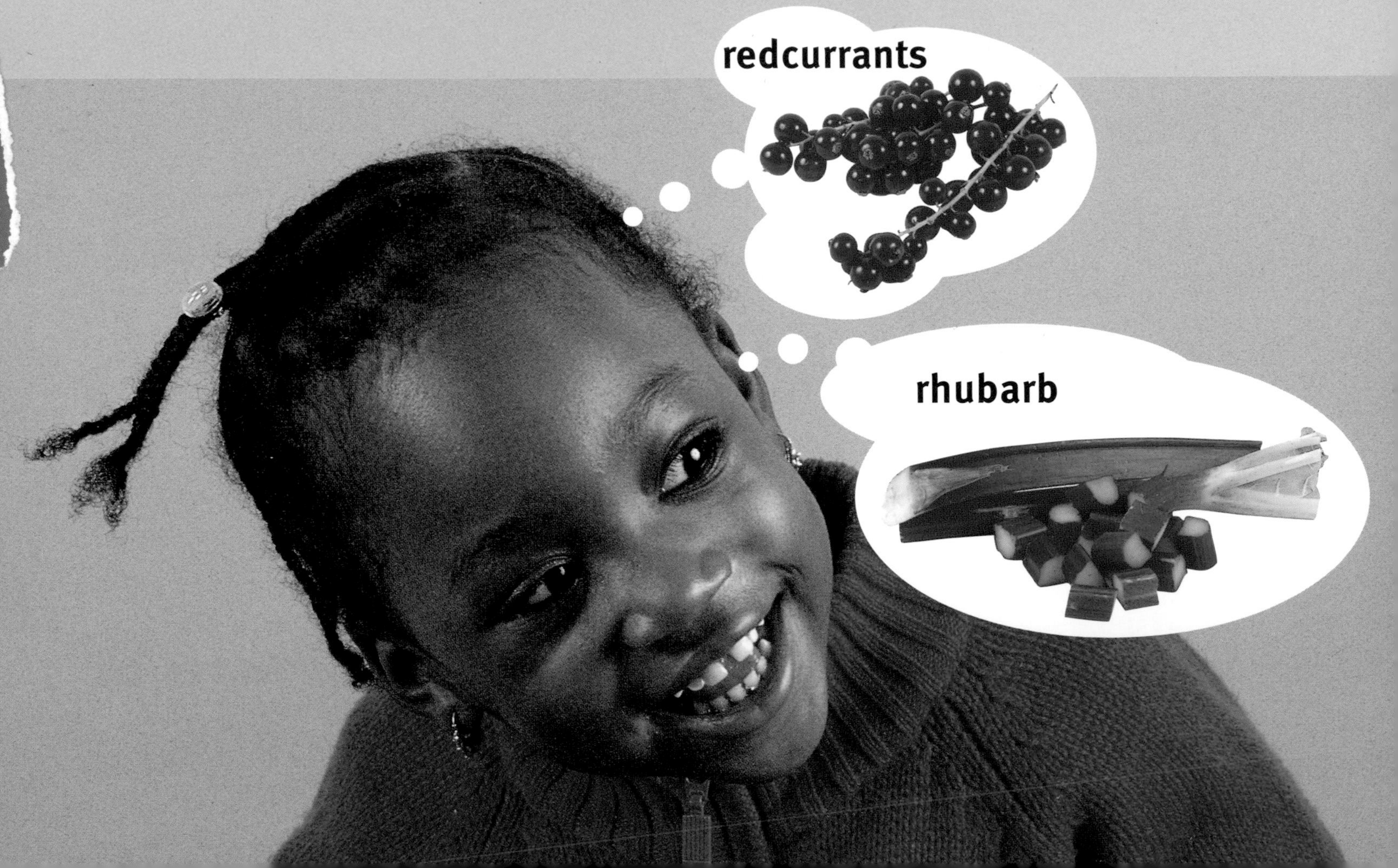

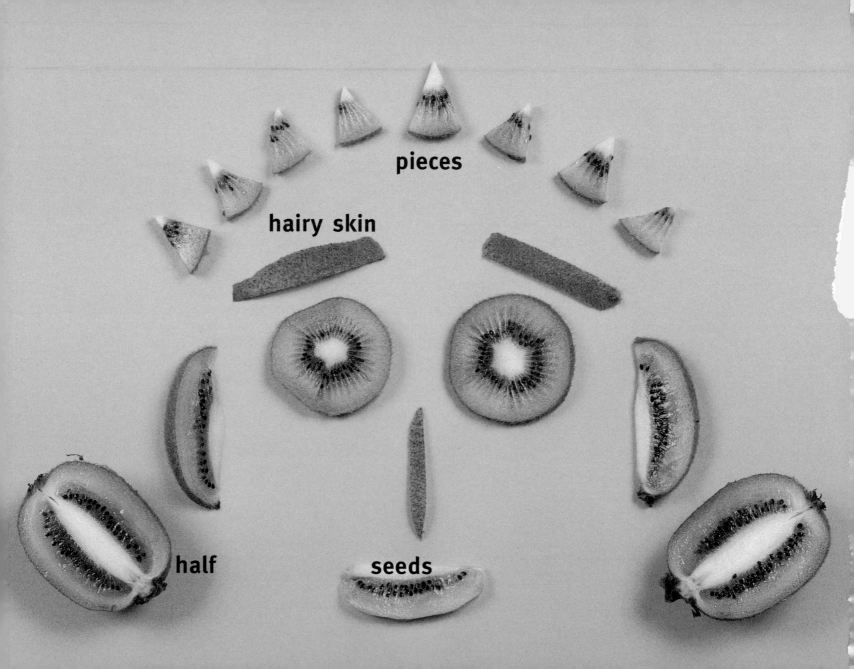

pieces

hairy skin

half

seeds

banana

sultanas

chewy and tasty like...

corn on the cob

dried
apricots

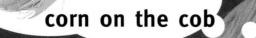

bagel

black grapes

currants: dried black grapes

bunches

white grapes

skin

half

sultanas: dried white grapes

coconut

large piece

sweet

coconut water

pieces

hairy shell

apple

strawberry

lemon